Praise for
"Thank You for Submitting Your Proposal"

"Since most decision-making inside foundations is a mystery only hinted at in annual reports or websites, the grantseeking public is left to wonder what actions could possibly be appropriate to help their cause. The answer is here."

> Jon Pratt, Executive Director
> *Minnesota Council of Nonprofits, St. Paul*

"Opens wide the closed doors behind which foundations make their secret and fateful funding decisions. Teitel condenses his decades of experience into an extraordinarily helpful guide for all those wishing to raise money."

> Robert Gass, Director of Training
> *Rockwood Leadership Program*
> *Berkeley, Calif.*

"A wise, experienced leader in the foundation world, always with a twinkle in his eye and an affection for people, gives us good plain advice for working with the world of foundations."

> Carter Roberts, President and CEO
> *World Wildlife Fund*

"Thoughtful, personal advice on how to get your proposal through the door, connect with foundation staff, and make the strongest possible case for funding the work you believe in."

> Brownie Carson, Executive Director
> *Natural Resources Council of Maine, Augusta*

"Offers a rare guided tour of foundation grantmaking from within. Martin Teitel's understanding of what's at stake and refusal to sugar-coat the odds drive a basic 'deal with it' message, which he delivers with humor, compassion, and stories."

> Monica Moore, Program Director
> *Pesticide Action Network*
> *North America Regional Center*

"Full of plain talk, practical insights, and wise advice from someone with experience on both sides of the funder table."

> Henry Holmes, Program Officer
> *The Columbia Foundation, San Francisco*

"Thank You for Submitting Your Proposal"

**A Foundation Director Reveals
What Happens Next**

First printed June 2006

10 9 8 7 6 5 4 3 2 1

Printed in the United States of America

This text is printed on 100% recycled, acid-free paper.

Emerson & Church, Publishers
P.O. Box 338, Medfield, MA 02052
Tel. 508-359-0019
Fax 508-359-2703
www.emersonandchurch.com

Library of Congress Cataloging-in-Publication Data

Teitel, Martin.
 "Thank you for submitting your proposal" : a foundation director reveals what happens next / Martin Teitel.
   p. cm.
  ISBN 1-889102-25-3 (pbk. : alk. paper)
  1. Proposal writing for grants. 2. Fund raising. I. Title.
 HG177.T45 2006
 658.15'224—dc22

                              2006000303

"Thank You for Submitting Your Proposal"

A Foundation Director Reveals What Happens Next

Martin Teitel

Foreword by Theodore M. Smith

Emerson
& Church
PUBLISHERS

DEDICATION

I met my wife the day I interviewed
for my first foundation job.
No grant, however large, can top that.

FOREWORD

In the revered rhetoric of American democracy, anyone can grow up to be president. In the equally grand tradition of America's private enterprise system, anyone can become a millionaire. Neither of these aphorisms is true, of course, because the playing field is never level.

Is the same true in the case of American philanthropy? Can anyone secure grants from the tax-protected dollars that foundations are legally required to dispense annually for charitable, educational or scientific purposes? Of course not!

The genius of Martin Teitel's book is that it is aimed at leveling the playing field for grantseekers. While he doesn't provide a key to the foundation's vault, he does pull back the curtain to expose much of what goes on inside American foundations – especially those that are professionally organized.

From an insider's perspective, this enjoyably presented exposé demystifies the business of dealing with grant applicants and grant proposals. With whimsy and plain street talk Teitel offers a stream of straight shots – do's and don'ts – drawn from his more than 30 years of experience.

I share Teitel's empathy for those trying to obtain foundation grants – as well as his dismay in seeing good ideas land on the cutting floor because of simple procedural mistakes by the applicants. It happens.

Look. If a foundation program officer receives 500 proposals during the year but has funding for only 50 grants, here are some good ways to *ruin your chances* of making the final 50. These practices do not guarantee failure, but I would give good odds on it.

• Ignore the foundation's guidelines that tell you precisely how to present your case for funding.

• Muddle or simply omit your intentions in the first paragraph of your cover letter.

• Assume that your ideas are so outstanding that they sell themselves and do not need to be *marketed* in a compelling way.

• Devote most of your proposal to an extended exposition of the problem, not to the solution(s).

• Create confusion about the strategy you are pursuing or just hide it.

• Above all, do not review the foundation's published list of grants over the last year.

As Teitel laments, even great ideas crash on procedural rocks. What a waste. The philanthropic market is probably no more rational than the American capitalist system with its winners and losers. And yet venture capital is essential to both if there is to be progress.

One great thing about the American philanthropic tradition is that there is indeed risk money to be found and if you develop a good strategy on an important societal challenge and can be persuasive, sooner or later you will likely gain support for it.

Whoever absorbs the sage counsel so generously offered in Teitel's well-grounded treatise will almost certainly improve his grantseeking success. If that is not your goal, give this book to a competitor, take a box seat, and watch while others benefit from its wily wisdom.

Theodore M. Smith   *Henry P. Kendall Foundation*
Executive Director

I've Looked at Life from Both Sides Now

Years ago, running a tiny nonprofit in San Francisco, I was on the phone with the electric company, trying to convince them to let us go another two weeks without paying our bill, until a hoped-for check arrived. I couldn't help it – as I pleaded with them my voice cracked, as if I were going to cry. We were given the extension.

When I looked up from the call, the other staff – all of whom were behind in being paid – quickly looked down at their work in embarrassment. I collected myself and announced, "In my next life, I'm going to be a funder."

Within a year, my prayers were answered, and I began the first of a number of jobs working for people who give money away, instead of those constantly seeking it.

I love the satisfaction of helping people who are doing wonderful things for other people, not to mention the regular paychecks. But I've never forgotten that San Francisco job, nor others I've held in the hardscrabble world of grantseeking nonprofits.

In this book, I want to share as openly and frankly as I can what it's like to be a funder. My hope is to provide tools that will help you increase your chances of getting the support you need.

In the almost 30 years since that awful day in San Francisco, I've met with an army of grantseekers, I've read many thousands of proposals, and I've had a hand in dispensing millions of dollars. Along the way I've learned a few things about what works – and what doesn't.

In my life as a funder, I've actually seen few proposals advocating for bad ideas. But I have encountered an astonishing number of funding requests that were cast in the worst possible light and even more that were clearly directed to the wrong funding source. For years I've thought about how much everyone, grantseekers and grantmakers alike, could benefit from some candid information.

When I sit down with my staff each week to review the latest crop of funding requests, what are we looking for? How do we really make our screening decisions? What is it like on the inside?

While I surely can't speak for all funders, I can share some of how the grantmaking process actually works for some of us. By doing so, I hope to help grantseekers as well as those of us who give money away, by increasing the chances that worthy funding requests end up in the right hands.

CONTENTS

1

Not-So Divided Loyalties: Whom Does the Funder Work For?

Our country finances itself by adopting a budget and then compelling its citizens to pay taxes to support what the government spends. When someone doesn't pay taxes, the rest of us have to pay a little more to compensate.

The 70,000 private foundations in our country pay very little in taxes – usually one or two percent of what they earn. And donors to foundations can deduct from their own tax bill the thousands or millions they contribute.

In exchange for this rather sweet deal with the government, foundations are required to spend their

19

money on "educational, scientific and charitable" purposes. In other words, they have to do something for the public good.

If you think this is pocket change, U.S. foundations have assets in excess of half a trillion dollars, resulting in $25 billion in grants.

Given that all of us who pay taxes undeniably pay more because of the billions that aren't fully taxed or taxed at all, we all should have an interest in what foundations do. Even, perhaps, in how they treat people – those taxpayers – who ask for money.

A few years ago, when I was raising money for a nonprofit group, I called a foundation officer in New York whom I knew from our mutual service on a committee. I told her I had a good idea for a project that fit the work she was doing. She asked me to put it in writing on one page and call her back in a few weeks.

Those of you who are experienced fundraisers know what's coming next. I called the program officer back in two weeks and asked what she thought of my letter. "What letter?" she barked. I persisted as inoffensively as possible, finally inducing her to look on her desk where she found the unread letter.

I told her I wouldn't mind in the slightest if she read it while I waited quietly on the phone (it had taken me two days to get through and I didn't want to hang up and start all over).

There was a long silence. Then she blurted out, "This

is stupid!" "Oh," I said brightly, as if she'd just offered to buy lunch, "What might I have left out?" "Well," she said, "you don't mention a single person I know. You can't possibly know what you're doing. Bye." Click. Not all foundation people are that unswervingly impolite. But those of you who have approached some of the 70,000 foundations know that there are nearly as many sets of guidelines and rules, and a huge variation in how people are treated, varying from well-mannered to creatively egregious.

Why worry about behavior and tax and accountability issues? What you really want to know is, how do I get the money?

The conundrum of funder accountability matters for two reasons. First, *you have a right* to ask for money: in a real sense, it's our society's money. And approaching the task of grantseeking can and should be based on your proceeding with your head held high, not groveling for largess, but requesting a share of a publicly-supported resource.

Second, the story about the one-page letter illustrates the other startling fact of foundation fundraising. Your morale and even sanity will be improved if you don't expect fairness, justice, or rationality – not to mention basic courtesy.

Fundraising is like what dating in high school was for some of us: hard work intertwined with great risk and continual rejection. It'll go better if you can find a way not to take it personally.

■ Who's In Charge Here?

I call on my foundation colleagues occasionally as I travel around visiting grantees and going to meetings. I get to see some pretty spiffy digs: cascading fountains in the lobbies, exquisite art, ergonomic conference room chairs, and the latest in computer hardware.

To be sure, some funding administrators work in modest surroundings. And, according to the Council on Foundation's annual compensation surveys, a number of them make even less than those employed at the agencies we fund.

But on the whole, working for a foundation is pretty darn nice: good pay, excellent fringe benefits, pleasant surroundings, sometimes even first class travel. It's easy to see how some people can begin to confuse their imposing surroundings with personal weightiness.

Aside from the perks, perhaps the greatest jeopardy to individual modesty in the funding business is something I touched on earlier: funders have lots of barely-accountable power. Having power doesn't mean it's abused, but having it does mean a person can come to feel they deserve it.

Back when I ran a foundation in California, we had a huge flow of proposals, so many that we had to buy big metal carts to wheel the weekly load up and down the hallway. And we had to add on to a storage building for all the file cabinets of paperwork. Out of all those thousands of proposals, we rejected 95 percent of them! The quick and simple act of coding a proposal for rejection meant that some hard-working group might not make payroll, or that a genuinely beneficial and worthy piece of work might never happen.

Making those heavy decisions all day can gradually convince a program officer that *her* judgment is what really matters, that *she* is the one who's actually shaping what happens out in the world, not those pesky grantees.

What this leads to is a well-known occupational hazard amongst funders: high-and-mightiness. Arrogance. Self-absorption. Few of us in the funding business attribute these qualities to ourselves, but almost every one of us can privately point to others who exemplify the famous egotism of the profession. I'm fine, but you ought to see *that other guy*.

The truth is far from what you see in the haughty demeanor and posh surroundings in many foundation offices. The reality is, many funders are far less powerful than we (or they) might believe.

In a few foundations, mostly clustered at the top of the asset range, program officers and executive directors actually do have real power to decide what the money is spent on. But in most foundations, actual power lies elsewhere, and funder strutting is mainly puffery.

This is important, because grantseekers focus a great

deal of attention on foundation staff – are they barking up the wrong tree?

According to federal and most state laws, the responsibility for deciding where a foundation puts its money rests with the board of directors. The board has other responsibilities too, like making sure funds are invested prudently, and that various federal and state rules are followed. Board members, and in some instances top staff, bear *personal* liability for the acts and omissions of the foundation.

I should know. I was held liable years ago when a foundation I headed employed for a brief period an inept bookkeeper who missed a federal payroll tax payment. By the time the government figured this out, the interest and fines had increased to $700.

As the legal "foundation manager," the IRS held me personally responsible, even though the bookkeeper was long gone and I had no idea she had missed the payment. I had to pay the missed taxes and penalties out of my own pocket, and the foundation was prohibited from reimbursing me.

From this story there are two lessons we can learn in trying to understand how foundations work. For one thing, foundation boards and top managers are forever being "admonished" by their lawyers and accountants.

We pay people in designer suits to come to our offices periodically and scare us into acting in a prudent way. And to the extent that bathing funders in this continuing stream of cautions makes them less likely to do foolish or even corrupt things, it's good for all of us. Yet it also makes funders conservative, risk-averse, and obsessed with avoiding scandal.

Grantseekers who approach foundations with a less than straightforward accounting of what they're up to, do so at great peril, as we'll see when we talk about proposals.

The other central fact of foundation boards is that while most hire staff to serve as a barrier between them and grantseekers, it is the board, not staff, that determines and enforces the foundation's funding guidelines.

This is the single most important fact you can know in dealing with foundation staff: no matter how important they act, no matter how lovely and imposing their surroundings, it's likely they are functionaries carrying out the decisions of other – invisible – people.

When I win the lottery and establish my own foundation, it'll give money to only the causes I favor. In the meantime, the foundation that employs me makes sure – via its board of directors – that I pay attention to the causes the foundation's donor, as interpreted by the board, wanted supported. I like those causes and I'm glad to help, but I'm not an independent agent – I represent a complex organization with its own history and standards.

Therefore, good foundation fundraising should begin, and in a sense end, with finding out what the board considers important: read the guidelines. No matter how quirky or even misguided those guidelines and strategies may seem, there really is no point in arguing. It only annoys the people you're trying to convince to help you.

In addition to the published guidelines, foundations always give you another valuable look into what they consider important: the grants list. This is where they've put their money: there is no more certain indicator of what a foundation actually cares about.

Nowadays many foundations list their grants on their web site, or they may publish a grants list, which they'll send you. If you must, get the foundation's federal tax Form 990-PF.

2

Let the Games Begin: Letters of Inquiry

One day, quite a few years ago, I went to see a colleague in a huge foundation on the west coast. I sat in the waiting room (yes, funders even keep other funders waiting) watching the receptionist work. In between answering the phone and greeting me, she snapped her gum and sorted through a stack of flat manila envelopes – obviously proposals.

The young woman would glance at the return address and the cover letter, and then enter information into her computer. Just about every foundation I know has some version of this process, logging in proposals so they can be tracked. The classic foundation form letters ("...while many proposals describe interesting and important work, we regret that limited funds...") are emitted from these databases of supplicants.

After logging in the proposal, the receptionist read a bit more on the first page, and with a few of the packets flipped back a page or two. Then, and my jaw still drops at the thought, *she tossed various proposals into the wastebasket next to her desk.* Every fifth or tenth one, she'd put into a folder and place it on top of a depressingly small stack on her desk.

I don't know who this young person was or her qualifications. Maybe she was the world's youngest Ph.D. in astrophysics and was simply covering the receptionist's desk for a while. It doesn't matter.

What I saw was what could have been days and weeks of work – an entire organization's hopes and plans and dreams – receiving fewer than 60 seconds of cursory screening (if screening is the word). And I have some reason to believe that while this particular foundation's screening technique seems a bit pitiless even in a normally hard-edged business, it is far from unique.

While I won't defend any funder who disrespectfully gives short shrift to the hard work of the world's proposal writers, those of us on the receiving end *can* point with exasperation to the enormous volume of junk proposals that wend our way.

People find or buy lists of funders, plug them into their database, and send out what must be immense numbers of generic proposals. Maybe once in a while this scattershot technique works. I suppose if you went to a mall looking for a ham sandwich, started at one end and went to every single store with your request, you might eventually stumble into a place that could fix you up – after having wasted the time of the puzzled clerks in The Sharper Image and Talbots.

Misplaced proposals waste the effort of busy grantseekers, and they also clog up the funder screening system. I have a friend who works for a foundation on the west coast. Whenever she succeeds in talking a prospective grantee out of submitting an inappropriate proposal, she hangs up the phone and rings a bell.

While no one keeps statistics about the internal workings of foundations, anecdotally it seems certain that more and more foundations are shunning these unsolicited proposals. Instead, a small number of foundations, especially those making huge grants or sizable hard science awards, send out RFP's: Requests for Proposals. The RFP's describe in some detail what will be funded and how to apply.

But for most foundations that shun unsolicited proposals, the standard technique is to require LOI's instead of RFP's (foundations rival the military in their love of acronyms).

LOI's – Letter of Inquiry – are an example of a genuine win-win situation. Foundations avoid an avalanche of paper, and grantees are spared writing and sending thick stacks of verbiage, charts, and testimonials.

A Letter of Inquiry distills the organization's request down to something quite brief. It gives the foundation an opportunity to express interest, and if the putative grantee has her ears open, a chance to say what tweaking of the idea might actually result in a grant.

Before we examine the LOI itself, let's look at how one foundation – the one I run – handles letters of inquiry. As an entirely quirky industry, foundations are quite free to invent whatever system suits their purposes. Some foundations use an intermediate step called a "pre-proposal"; some have quite different standards for how they define and handle LOI's. So what I'm describing here is just an example.

The person whose job includes opening the mail pulls out what appear to her to be LOI's. You're about to encounter the only sports metaphor you'll read in this entire book, for which I apologize. My rule for many years has been, "The tie goes to the runner."

How we understand this rule in foundation-land is, if we're not sure something is actually a Letter of Inquiry, we treat it like one. A bit later we'll return to this point, since you might be surprised to learn how difficult it is for us dense funders to read the minds of grantseekers.

At any rate, the person opening the mail records the basic information of the LOI in a very simple database, and addresses and mails a pre-printed postcard that essentially says: We received your Letter of Inquiry. If we want to know anything more about it we'll contact you, otherwise you won't hear from us again.

Lest you think sending this acknowledgment is a rare instance of funder courtesy, be assured that while many of us are fans of good manners, the card's main purpose is to drastically reduce the volume of calls asking, "Did you get what I sent you?"

The U.S. Postal Service is stunningly efficient and I'm not aware of any of those calls actually enlightening us. But the impulse to telephone and make sure the LOI arrived is entirely understandable. Thus our postcard.

Now enshrined in a folder, the Letter of Inquiry is passed to a program officer for review. A very bright and well qualified young man, in the case of our office, has this particular task in his job description because – I promised to be honest with you – he has the least seniority in the organization.

The fact that foundation staff don't like to process LOI's is useful information to know, and we're going to return to this when we construct the road map to a successful Letter of Inquiry.

The program officer then reads the LOI. Yes, he really does. As he reads, he pulls up a pre-made Excel spreadsheet and pecks at it, filling in basic information such as the topic of the proposal, the essential strategy being used, and a *one sentence* summary of the Letter of Inquiry. Did you get that? Your complex and subtle organization's life, already stripped of nuance by being reduced to a three-page LOI, is now further condensed to a tiny box on a spreadsheet.

When a week or two have gone by, the program officer emails the spreadsheet to his boss, the deputy director, and to me. (In a larger foundation more people might be in the loop, but not necessarily, say my colleagues, since foundations with bigger bucks are often organized into departments – mine is not.)

The young man's covering email respectfully cajoles us to read the spreadsheet prior to arriving at our regular weekly program meeting. While many of us are fans of Letters of Inquiry, we don't always like the process of going through them, as it's a bit like panning for gold: you have to sort through an awful lot of gravel before coming upon that little bright flash.

On Wednesday morning, we put our coffee mugs on the conference room table and the young man thumps down the stack of LOI's. By then I've probably printed out my copy of the spreadsheet and scribbled a bit on it, trying my hardest not to pre-judge based on the barest of summaries.

The program officer leads us through the list, in the order on the spreadsheet, which means in the order received. He tells us the name of the proposal in his hand. Often, everyone chirps, "Nope, not a fit." The program officer makes a note in the "outcome" box on his spreadsheet, and we move on. It's over in five seconds.

But occasionally one of us says, "Let me look at that."

Something in the strategy box or the topic of the proposed work is interesting. If I'm the one asking to see the paperwork, I'll usually glance first at the letterhead if it has an advisory panel or board of directors listed. After that I'll flip right to the budget, ignoring the cover letter.

At other times an idea catches fire in our little meeting, and people start to pass the folder around and point out aspects of the proposed work that interest us. This can result in the LOI being assigned to one of us for further investigation.

My role as Curmudgeon-in-Chief is also to stop us from getting too fired up. I often say, "I agree this is a neat idea. Can anyone sitting here really picture our board voting for a grant to something this far from our guidelines?" All right, the nays have it.

In a typical batch of 20 Letters of Inquiry, it would be ordinary for two to be flagged for follow-up. But it wouldn't be remarkable for there to be none. When this happens, the staff kind of drag out of the meeting, disappointed.

Let me tell you something about foundation staff, and I've been acquainted with quite a few over the years. We like working on proposals, we like making grants. Contrary to what my children will tell you, saying "no" isn't my greatest pleasure in life. I bring this up to emphasize the fact that your success in getting a grant is linked to your ability to constructively connect with someone *who is already inclined to help.*

Let's leave these funders to their now-cold coffee, and turn our focus more directly to the art and science of Letters of Inquiry.

Let me start with a piece of advice that won't exactly floor you. If the foundation has published guidelines or suggestions for how they want an LOI, follow them with precision, even (and especially) if they're called suggestions or guidelines rather than rules.

I'm not saying you should do this because I'm a great fan of rules, or because I love rubbing the faces of grantees in the inherent power imbalance existing between foundations and grantseekers. Rather, I want you to get your funding. And the foundation is actually telling you what to do to get it.

Your version of what the guidelines should be might indeed be better. You might be able to tell your story better in six pages rather than the required three. You might have some great video footage even though the guidelines say, Don't send media.

It doesn't really matter who knows best, at least at this early point in the process. Your purpose is not to reform, it's to get in the door and get some money. You can impress the foundation with your creativity later. For now, follow what is suggested with the precision of a Swiss watchmaker.

One last thing before we move on to the LOI's content. Please understand that we foundation people struggle with perceiving what it is you're trying to tell us. So rather than have us guess whether you're sending information or actually entering into the grantseeking process (you see, we're on lots and lots of mailing lists), type Letter of Inquiry at the top of what you send. Not only will it please the screener, it'll get you one step closer to your goal. And that goal is to provoke an invitation to submit a proposal – that's all.

Now on to content.

A typical LOI will have a title, a one- or two-sentence summary of the entire project, an explanation of the issue being addressed and how, and a description of the organization doing the work. In my foundation, a budget is always attached. Foundations vary in their requirements, but three pages plus the budget is a typical Letter of Inquiry. What you really have here is a proposal, in miniature.

Something that seems to characterize many of the decent and good-hearted people who work for nonprofits is that they're quite interested in telling you about their work: what it involves, and why it's interesting. They will tell you, and tell you, and tell you. With LOI space so very limited, verbosity is a real problem.

What I've observed is that grantee enthusiasts, faced with the task of constructing a three-page Letter of Inquiry, make one of two mistakes – sometimes both. They either give themselves permission to write four or five or 10 pages, because they're convinced they can capture the funder's attention, or they take their 20-page proposal and hack away until it's three pages long – and entirely unintelligible.

What is needed instead is concise and powerful prose that evokes the content and spirit of the project in a very small space. This is not a shorter version of the full proposal, but actually a different piece of writing that fulfills a distinctive function.

Let's go through the elements of a typical Letter of Inquiry, starting with the title of your work.

Suppose you're a group of soccer parents who want to work with several local school systems. Your hope is that they will adopt integrated pest management practices instead of spreading nasty chemicals on the fields where your kids run around after school every day.

So you could indeed send out a funding request called, "Integrating Contemporary Pest Management and Soil Amendment Regimes in Outdoor Recreation Facilities for School-Age Children and Other Young Citizens in Middlesex County." Or you could call what you're doing "The Safe Soccer League." Or "The Organic Sports Federation."

Whatever you call it, make it brief and catchy: the single purpose of the name of your project, in your Letter of Inquiry, is to induce the screener to read further. That's all. It's not to make the case or argue your brief. That can come later, if your LOI isn't languishing in the wastebasket.

Let's move on to the summary. Some people call this the elevator speech: how you tell someone the totality of what you're doing while riding between the 4th floor and the lobby. This is really hard for many people.

The summary has three standards, and you must achieve all three of them:

• Concise – every word must count,

• Compelling – no vacuous buzzwords,

• Clear – eliminate any chance of ambiguity or misreading.

Many years ago I ran an international relief program with teams of people all over the world. With no phone service, and letters taking weeks to arrive, we relied on cables – international telegrams. The cables were quite expensive and had to be concise, often limited to under a dozen words.

We spent a lot of time constructing exceptionally succinct messages that left no room for mistakes in interpretation. Giving people instructions about what to do next in war zones can't leave room for doubt.

A normally loquacious person, I was challenged by this part of my job. Here are some lessons I learned in those pre-Internet days, and subsequently from many years of reading funding request summaries:

1) Your central and first step is to ask a question – sometimes a group of people can do this together: "What,

in one brief sentence, are we doing?"Answering a question seems to help, and groups often come up with the right words when one person is stuck.

2) If you put 50 percent of your LOI effort into the summary, half of that effort should be directed towards writing a brilliant opening sentence. I actually mean this. If you earmark four hours for writing your Letter of Inquiry, then you should work on the summary for two hours, an hour of which is just laboring over, and coming back to, that first sentence.

3) Learn from, but don't emulate, professional marketers. That is, make your prose interesting, even riveting. But don't write something that sounds like you're selling soap powder. Like professional marketers, you need to know your audience, and then create a tone best suiting your purpose. You want the foundation to "buy" your product, but without seeming like your goal is selling instead of creating a partnership.

4) Avoid the sticky pit of buzzwords. Don't claim your work is "unique," or "cutting edge," or "raises awareness." Words and phrases like these are (a) unsupported general claims, or (b) impossible to know or verify. And beware of flowery adjectives and vague generalities. These don't create an impression of competence and they won't cause your LOI to stand out from the pile of pithy prose.

5) Instead, let your summary be filled with facts, concrete verbs, and sentences that show action. Emulate the writing of good journalists in mainstream newspapers: be an objective-seeming reporter who lets his words create a response, rather than manipulating, exhorting, or lecturing the reader.

To illustrate a few of these points, let's stay with my imaginary example from above, which comes to mind since in real life I do live across from a soccer field. Which of these entirely fictional LOI summaries works better for you?

A) This innovative program seeks to make a unique contribution to the field of lawn care and athletic field husbandry while maintaining a health-inducing atmosphere for soccer players and providing a unique opportunity to meet our goals and objectives in addressing the scourge of chemical companies world-wide and making chemistry information available to the entire country through our model project.

B) The State Department of Health says that as many as 1,000 young people are poisoned by lawn chemicals each year. Our organization is protecting children who play on the county's athletic fields by adopting a list of 57 safe and effective methods of sports field care.

Choice A is wordy, a combination of vague and

inflammatory terms, and is really beside the point. After slogging through A, the program officer may still be unclear about what's going on – provided by the end of that impossibly lengthy sentence she's still awake.

Choice B starts with a grabber (which I made up, don't pull your kid out of soccer). The second sentence then says what you're going to do – enough to paint a picture but not enough to thwart the reader's interest in learning more. The other thing about that sentence is that its claims are modest, quite positive, and there's no blame or finger-pointing.

Since I bring it up, let me say a quick word about finger-pointing. People seeking grants are often solving problems, and problems have causes. You can't talk about poverty, spousal abuse, illness or other serious problems without acknowledging that in many instances one component of dealing with the problem is eliminating its cause.

That's all true. But in your summary, you need to use positive language to draw the reader in (you can get to the tougher stuff in the body of the LOI, or in your full proposal if you're invited to submit one). Because you have to be so concise, and you might not know exactly who is reading your Letter of Inquiry, err on the side of being more positive by focusing on what you will be doing, less on who is to blame.

OK, you have constructed that excellent summary, which will be as long or as short as required by your very careful reading of the funder's LOI requirements. Now you have to write the body of the piece. This isn't easy, but it is easier than many tasks in fundraising.

Unlike the summary of your work, which needs to be specially thought about and written, the body of your LOI can be a boiled down version of your proposal – in some respects it can function like an outline of your full-blown proposal and budget.

Unless the funder has special requirements, such as a list of questions or a web-based form to fill out, you simply need to fit your project description into the space you're permitted.

Before closing out this chapter, let me offer one last piece of advice. Take a Post-It note and write on it, "My goal is to have a proposal invited." Stick the note on your computer monitor, and refer to it often.

Every single word in your Letter of Inquiry needs to be held up to this test and this test only. Don't use the LOI to make grand-scale points about the state of the world, show your erudition or wit, or argue the fascinating minutiae of soccer field care.

Single-mindedness in LOI writing is no vice; your only goal is to get that call from the foundation staff person, asking for more.

With that admonishment in mind, let's move now to the fun stuff: writing the proposal that results in a grant.

3

Meat and Potatoes: Proposals and Budgets

Today is deadline day at the foundation. While a handful of people have sent in their proposals early (undoubtedly the same ones who sat in the first row in junior high), on this day the FedEx man is wheeling a cart to haul the incoming stack of proposals. I've seen this many times, by the way. Deadline day at a foundation can indeed trigger Christmas-like tactics on the part of suddenly taxed delivery services.

Once received, the envelopes are opened, the proposals entered into a computer log and, often, assigned a tracking number. The various odd pieces – sample brochures, tapes, CD's, clippings and the like – are enshrined in files or bins or some method of (not always flawless) retention. Whatever the quirks of the foundation's system, eventually the proposal finds its way to the desk of a program officer.

There she sits, a ceramic mug of coffee in her hand to combat the dreaded occupational disease of program officers: MEGO. The term refers to a condition caused by reading scores if not hundreds of proposals in a brief span of time. It stands for My Eyes Glaze Over.

As a proposal writer, know that your first and main job is to avoid inducing an acute case of MEGO. Your goal is to get that program officer to assign a code to your proposal that keeps it alive in the evaluation and screening system. You have no other goal.

After several decades of poring over proposals, I want to share some overall tips with you, before we drill down to proposal specifics.

1) In general, I think people are drawn to follow those with solutions, not troubles. The old conventional wisdom had a proposal starting with a "problem statement." While many organizations are indeed trying to address a serious problem, I've seen far too many proposals that are almost all problem statement, with scant information about just what you're going to do to remediate your organization's major concern. The key here is to inspire with a vision, and impress with a credible action plan.

2) Part of the job of inspiring the funder is to write clearly. Avoid jargon and technical terms unless you're seeking funding for a technical project like scientific research and are certain the reader of the proposal will understand what you're talking about. Similarly, use metaphor sparingly – save the purple prose for that novel chronicling your fundraising angst.

And use statistics like hot pepper: a little goes a long way. If you must go into six pages of detailed charts on some statistical trend, and the foundation's rules permit it, put that wonky stuff into an appendix, so you don't give the reader good cause to give up reading in the middle. Even this book puts the lists in a separate section (see Part Two – The Grantseeker's Reality Check). Keep it flowing: short sentences that draw the reader in are usually best.

3) Here's a hot tip: don't threaten the funder. Years ago, during the height of the Cold War, I received a proposal from a major east coast university asking for $10,000 to fund a conference of academics to talk about the possibility of nuclear war.

While I was sympathetic with the issue of preventing global holocaust, and even then $10,000 wasn't that much money, I didn't see the use of having a group of scholars sit around for a couple of days and wring their hands together – there was no action component in the proposal other than jaw-boning. So I politely declined and promptly forgot about it.

Several weeks later, my phone buzzed and I was told the president of this university was on the phone. He was a distinguished scholar with a world-wide reputation. Having totally forgotten about my five minutes with his school's proposal, I took the call and began by inquiring after his health. He wasted no time, retorting, "Mr. Teitel, there will be global thermonuclear war, and it will be your fault." Click.

While not as colorful, many proposal writers make that same mistake of thinking blackmail or guilt is the route to a foundation's checkbook. They think emotional manipulation is an effective tool. I want to tell you emphatically that it is not.

There is no reason to avoid a concise description of the real problems and issues in the world, but it's counter-productive to lay responsibility for fixing the problem at the feet of the funder. It won't help you get money. What should you do instead? Read what comes next:

4) Over many years, I've learned to spot proposals that correlate with successful work. Instead of informing me that if our foundation doesn't give you money something awful will happen, or that if we don't fund you, you might go out of business, better proposals say this: "We are doing something wonderful here, and we're going to do it with or without you. With you, it will

happen faster and better – but it's happening nonetheless. Please join us in this excellent work."

I heard a panel of venture capitalists recently; they are sister funders after all. And they said exactly the same thing. They can recognize the businesses they should invest in by just the same kinds of statements in the business plans that function as proposals in the VC world.

5) It often happens in the course of your funding research, especially with small or local foundations, that you find you know someone on the board, or someone who goes to church with that person, or has a kid on their soccer team. So you figure, I'm going to use this advantage, and go right to that person, because I read in Chapter 1 that board members make the funding decisions, not staff.

There are two good reasons to resist this temptation, unless you have very specific and concrete information that such an approach is welcome and encouraged.

The first is that many foundation board members expect their staff to buffer them from being hassled. As you would imagine, people try hard to reach the decision-makers, because they want to make the case for a grant in-person. But while you're no doubt correct in assuming that you're fascinating in your personal portrayal of the problems of the day, and charming in your manner, you run a serious risk of annoying just the person you hope will end up liking your work. And as for charm, the funding decision is about your organization and its work: the judgment to make a grant isn't likely to be based on your personality.

The other reason not to do what we call the "end run" is the risk it creates with foundation staff. I don't actually know anyone who enjoys having a person go over his or her head. The board member you're chatting merrily with at the party is my boss. It won't hurt to keep the funding world's hierarchy in mind.

If you really do find yourself standing at the soccer sidelines screaming at your kids alongside a foundation board member whose kid is on the same team, find a casual way to let the foundation staff know you have that connection, and you're not exploiting it. Keep the foundation staff as allies – that's the surest route to a check.

6) One more piece of advice before we get down to the basics of actually writing a proposal. Use the cut-and-paste function in your word processor, but use it skillfully.

While some foundations have application forms and some ask very, shall we say idiosyncratic, questions, in general there are only so many ways you can describe your organization and its activities. Given the convenience of modern software, there's an understandable tendency to delay writing the proposal until a day or two before the deadline, knowing you can load an old proposal and just stitch and glue until you have something that seems to meet the requirements. While it's OK to use a basic proposal for all the variations you need to produce, be very careful about leaving out transitions and connective tissue, and conversely about repetition and redundancy.

Most of us have a natural tendency to mentally fill in those pesky leaps of logic and narrative that can make the difference between a ho-hum proposal and something that compels. And every few months I receive a proposal addressed to other funders or foundations, due to rushed editing of a generic proposal.

4

Writing a Wonderful Proposal

Proposals vary widely, from ponderous tomes meant to produce millions of dollars of research funds over many years to simple, eloquent pleas for help. I once funded a group that made their request on a postcard. Still, you can divide most funding requests into five basic components, even though you may need to adjust for individual circumstances:

The Summary – something between a paragraph and a page (check the guidelines before you start) that does a masterful job of meeting the "Three C's" standard: clear, concise, and compelling.

The Vision – known in the Dark Ages as the problem

statement, this section describes the issue you're addressing, and why it's important you do so.

Strategies and Tactics – this is where the verbs leap off the page. You say *exactly* what you're going to do that will change something in the real world.

Resources – what will support your strategies and tactics? This section should include every resource: people, money, time, and material. Don't make the mistake of just talking about money, although finances are a major concern.

Fundamentals – this part sometimes resides in appendices or at the end of the proposal, but is no less important. It includes items like your tax determination letter as well as other bits and pieces either required by the funder or that you feel confident are welcome, such as a list of your board members, letters of recommendation, and samples of successful work.

With that said, let's now look more closely at each of these five components.

■ The Summary

Everything we said about writing a summary for a Letter of Inquiry applies here, but much more so.

It's a major mistake to think the word "summary" actually requires you to summarize your work by simply restating it in fewer words. Unnaturally compressed writing is rarely compelling. Instead, step back and think hard about your elevator speech: how would you tell someone about your work in a minute or less? Organizations that use door-to-door or telephone canvassers are usually good at this – they know they need to be complete *and* persuasive in the few seconds before the door gets slammed.

When I sit down at my desk and start pulling proposals off the stack, I start with the summary. Here is what I'm looking for:

1) I automatically search for key words I can connect to what my foundation funds.

2) I try to discern a beginning, a middle, and an end to the proposed work. That is, is there a logical flow of strategies and resources so that by the end of the project something will have been accomplished that I can see and maybe even measure?

3) A more subtle feature I'm alert to is competence: do I get the impression that this is a going concern, a group of people who know what they're doing and why? Do I smell success?

4) And finally, I defend myself by casting an eye out for red flags – signs that there's a problem with the group, the strategies, or the resources. For example, my eye will stop rather quickly at the word "lobbying," since that

can be an issue between private foundations and the IRS. Or I might pause at an innocent word I know will be a fatal flaw with my particular foundation. In our case, we don't fund outside the U.S. If someone's summary talks about their excellent work in Sri Lanka, I know I can stop reading. This is where I uncover the folks who didn't look up my foundation's guidelines.

There is a more global standard – which we'll get to a bit later in more detail – that permeates my reading of each proposal. By the time I'm done, I want to know what will be different when this work is completed, and how will I know it? If I don't put down the proposal with a pretty good grasp of the project's impact, I'm going to have a difficult time being its advocate with my board.

This might be a good place to mention presentation. If you're applying to a foundation that requires submissions on paper, rules for resumes apply here: avoid cute fonts, tiny margins, colorful papers, and binding methods that stymie attempts to file or photocopy your work. And if you're applying online or emailing a proposal, avoid unique fonts and oddball formatting. Keep it simple, dignified, and accessible – make it easy for the funder to love you.

■ The Vision

Most proposals, after the summary, tell the reader what the grantseeking group is working on and why. This is your chance to soar – to wax compelling, and to show you know your stuff. In this section, three problems tend to surface, all of which you can easily avoid.

The number one flaw is that people go on way too long about the problem. My theory is that proposal writers care deeply about their work, and want to make sure you share their sense of urgency. So they go on and on and on.

Think of a brand new father and his 72 pictures of little Stephanie. Instead, go for quality. Select what tells your story in a vivid way – not flowery or overly dramatic, just persuasive. And let good, clear, strong words work for you. Quantity doesn't indicate consequence. Windiness more likely leads straight to MEGO.

The second common difficulty in talking about the vision is that people often leave out why the issue is important to them. This seems so self-evident to dedicated souls that they don't elaborate. But never squander an opportunity to explain why people in your organization are involved: connect vision and motivation. This is a key point of selling.

For example, if I'm writing a proposal for the Committee to Reduce Non-Stick Cookware, you might not know from our goal of decreasing non-stick items whether we're idiosyncratic chefs, people concerned about the possible health effects of these coatings, or folks who know that out-gassing from overheated non-stick pots and pans can be fatal to birds. If the foundation

I'm approaching has a funding category covering animal health, then making sure to say that my organization is composed of bird lovers links our group's vision to the foundation's purpose.

The third pitfall in writing about your core issues is actually a tough one. You need to talk clearly about what you're trying to change, but not drown the reader in an abyss of negativity and despair. If you're dealing with one of the many difficult and possibly even horrible issues in our world, then you should say so. Be clear and don't pull punches. But avoid wallowing and going on and on.

Going back to the days of possible nuclear confrontation between the United States and the USSR, one "peace" proposal I read consisted of many pages of stark detail about the effects of nuclear explosions on human beings, including two pages of melting eyeballs and burning flesh.

Tucked in at the end were some general statements about the need for people to pay attention to this danger. There was no hope, no vision of a world that was improved and what it might look like, and very little about how we might get to a better place.

This is why I try to avoid the term "problem statement," and instead focus on vision. Give the reader some reason to feel hopeful and positive; provide them with concrete indications that you're a problem solver, not just a problem describer.

■ Strategies and Tactics

People hate this part, and I don't blame them. If you aren't the shy type, stand on a street corner and ask passers-by the difference between a strategy and a tactic. It isn't intuitive for most people. Yet every group asking for money has a strategy and every group uses tactics to make that strategy work. If you don't say what those things are in your case, you risk confusion, and you might be passing up a significant place to connect with your prospective funder.

A strategy is the way you mobilize resources to achieve your goals. Tactics are the things you do with your mobilized resources. Let's look at an example.

If your organization is concerned about the plight of homeless people in big cities in the winter, your strategy might be to intervene directly with people on the street in cold weather. Your tactic might be to send around volunteers in vans to bring people indoors and also to pass out blankets.

Strategies are always choices.

Another group concerned about homeless people might use a different strategy: they might work with the people in city hall to achieve more funding for services for these individuals. Another organization might provide food, while another might try to change the housing laws so that people don't end up on the street in the first place.

If I'm a funder with guidelines that say I want to support organizations working on homeless issues, I need to know your strategy. Otherwise, I can't tell you apart from the other groups, or it might appear to me that you're rhetorical and unfocussed, so I won't want to provide funding. Don't hide your (strategic) light under a bushel.

When possible, connect your strategy to your vision with an iron chain. A really good strategy flows from and is even necessitated by the vision. Your vision statement might have a good deal to say about why it's important to reduce the root cause of problems, and why prevention is the best use of resources. And if you then say you're working in the statehouse to eliminate the causes of homelessness, your vision is linked to your strategy.

And be very careful here, by the way, to make your case in a strong way without appearing to denigrate others who make different strategic choices. The prospective funder might have just made a huge grant to the folks you're criticizing. Change in the world usually comes about when people with different strategies work on a difficult problem from many angles in a cooperative way – and funders know this.

Just as your strategy should flow from your vision, your tactics should be a natural consequence of your strategy. If you're working with city hall to change the rules, then it makes more sense to talk about your deployment of expert advocates in the civic process, not the blankets you pass out. Keep it logical, because you're aiming for that light bulb moment when the funder looks up from your proposal and says, "Oh, now I get it!"

■ Resources

We'll get to the budget in a moment, because that's everybody's focus. But make sure you account for *all* the resources you're going to deploy in your work. I am impressed when a group says, "We have a staff of three that represents a total of 46 years of experience in this field."

I take notice when a group working to change the laws about health care has two doctors, an insurance company executive and three street-level health care advocates on its board. Those are resources.

I also look for reasonable use of resources. If you have three staff and are aiming to make a major change in the ways things are in an entire state, I'm going to raise my eyebrows when your timeline promises results in three months.

Showing all the resources and how they'll be efficiently used impresses the reader, and it's indicative of good planning. Also some groups have resources particular to them, for example the organization passing out blankets to homeless people on cold nights might have two staff, but they can show an ongoing roster of

88 volunteers. This is notable, whereas only mentioning two staff raises the question of how the work could possibly get done.

Keep everything connected: your tactics should be entirely supported by your use of resources. No funder should read a proposal and say, 'How are they ever going to do that?" Inventory all of your resources – the people, the material you might have, the time you spend on your work, community support, and less tangible factors like artistic creativity or a history of strong community good will.

And then there is money.

The first part of a good money plan explains how you're going to secure the financial resources to accomplish your task. Again, this part of your proposal should connect clearly to your vision and your strategies and tactics.

If you claim strong community support for your work with homeless people in cold weather, one measure of this claim is your large number of volunteers. Another is your ability to show you have 300 contributors in your community. While the dollar amount is important, what best supports your claim of community involvement is how many local people are involved. Say so.

Even though you're approaching a foundation, be sure to indicate how you'll secure all of the non-foundation resources necessary to propel your work forward. A good program officer wants to locate her niche in your funding ecology.

You might say, "We're able to keep going with our base of 300 supporters in the community, our annual auction, and our cookie sales. But experience has shown us that the number of people who spend the winter on the street is increasing by 10 percent per year, while our fundraising efforts only grow by four percent per year, which is usual for small community groups of our type. Therefore, we're adding in a component of funding from local companies, which we think can raise half of the shortfall, and we're looking to our local foundation community to make up the rest."

You see the strength of this kind of statement? It shows you have a solid base, a reasonable plan that appears to have been researched and thought out, and your request of the foundation is both appropriate and compelling. Here is a chance for the funder to make a measurable difference by joining and enhancing your success.

The second part of the money plan is your budget. Start with an impeccable reading of the foundation's guidelines and do exactly as they say. Foundations are financial institutions, and often are picky about money and how it's accounted for.

Aside from compliance with the foundation's budget format, be sure to cover absolutely everything. Don't permit the program officer to say, "Well fine, but where in the budget is the cost of those blankets they're passing out?" List donations, in-kind contributions unless the foundation says not to – in fact show how you're budgeting for every single penny.

If your proposal is for $14.5 million a year for five years for cancer research, then you'll probably have plenty of pages of professionally prepared spreadsheets. But I doubt many people in that situation are reading this book.

A typical nonprofit trying to show how the money will be spent should appear professional and on top of the money, but also be clear, legible, and organized in ways that make sense to an ordinary person. Presentation matters a lot in spreadsheets and budgets – MEGO sets in early. Use notes and explanatory sections sparingly, because you don't want to appear defensive. But do explain what is not self-evident.

And now here is the secret trick in preparing budgets for foundations. Commit this to memory. Many foundation boards have a person on them, often the treasurer, who whiles away the long boring parts of the board meeting by checking your math. I can always spot this individual because she or he uses a pencil, never ink. And all too often the labor of these math checkers is rewarded.

I am not unsympathetic. I picture you, late at night, having spilled coffee into your computer keyboard for the second time, and your back is aching. You have changed the numbers in your budget 11 times. So you slip up a little. No blame, right?

Wrong. Fast-forward six months to the board meeting, where the treasurer is thundering, "You expect us to fund these people who aren't even competent enough to add a simple column of figures? Forget it!" You've killed your funding chances for a dumb reason, and to make matters worse, you've made your principal ally, your program officer or foundation executive director, look foolish. Not a sterling career move.

Yet it happens again and again, especially in smaller foundations that don't have the people-power to check your math for you. Budgets that don't add up are a common problem.

I said there were three things to your money section: first, an overview and context about how you will secure money to carry out your work; second, a budget; and lastly something that's a bit difficult to present: a concrete plan for what you'll do if you don't raise your budget.

This is a touchy subject, because it's hardly a hallmark of good selling to dwell on failure. But you simply must be prepared with a cogent answer to the question, "What will you do if you can't raise all the money in your plan?" I ask this question a lot and am frequently met with a deer in the headlights look.

Here is why you need to think about this. First of all, foundation board members love this question. They look at the fact that your budget is $500,000 and you only can account for $300,000 in fairly secure income. So they want to know, is your organization a going concern? And if they do make a grant, but all the money isn't there, will the foundation's money have been wasted?

A related issue is that the foundation, either at the staff or board level, might be hard-pressed for money, which believe it or not happens a lot. We might sit down at a board meeting and know we have about $2 million to spend during this particular funding round. But we might have $3 million in excellent proposals sitting before us.

We could just rank them in order of preference and draw a line when we run out of money. But often funders will attempt to reduce the amount granted to many of the groups on the grounds that some money is better than none.

Assuming you agree that you would rather have less money rather than zero, be prepared to help out, but don't volunteer this information. If you need $30,000 to round out the budget for your blankets for the homeless work and the foundation staff says, what if you only got $20,000, you shouldn't cry, say you will go out of business, or that you'll wing it.

A good answer might be, "We could still make good use of that reduced amount by cutting out one delivery crew to save overhead and asking the other volunteers to work an extra hour per night. And we would also hope to make up the money from local stores and companies."

Rehearse this answer; be ready. I can always tell when someone is faking it, and my purpose in asking it isn't to harass but to help. Yet I can't do much good with an incoherent or unconvincing response.

■ Fundamentals

When it comes to compiling proposal end matter, Hamlet would have been good at this: "Use all gently." As with other matters, I suggest you first check with the foundation's specifications, before adding in goodies to your proposal package.

My guess is that people work on this part of the proposal when they're the most tired, and maybe rushing to meet the FedEx deadline. Thus my staff makes phone call after phone call asking people to supply their IRS tax determination letter, even though I don't know of a single foundation that doesn't require it.

On the other hand, many organizations include thick bundles of testimonial letters. I read one occasionally, but in general I look at reference letters as an unnecessary assault on our tree supply, since I rather doubt that fundraisers would include letters from people who think the group does a bad job. It's like getting a reference from your mother: nice, but a bit predictable.

News clippings fall somewhere in the middle. You're unlikely to include clippings about the indictment of your group's treasurer. Still, a press account sometimes illustrates your competency in a project that relies on public education, or demonstrates that you have indeed plowed new ground – when the plowing of new ground is one of the objectives of your work.

As for your board of directors, list them unless the funder tells you not to. And include unusual or interesting work products or illustrations of your success.

Overall, use the same standard that has permeated this chapter: include anything that strengthens the connections among the various elements of your proposal, as well as items that add to the proposal in a specific, concrete manner. Leave out puffery and irrelevancies. When in doubt, don't.

Before we close this chapter, I have one final item, and some last cautions to share.

More and more funders are concerned about metrics: specific measurements of outcomes. Many dedicated people bridle at this requirement, fearing that quantifying their work omits the high quality they achieve. They want us to see that they not only pass out an average of 190 blankets each cold night to homeless people, but they also make those people feel less isolated, less hopeless, and more connected to other human beings.

In reporting on what you did with the grant – and you ignore the grant reporting chapter in this book at your considerable risk – there is a place for talking about those less material features of your work. But you really must comply with the request to measure your work.

If the funder provides a metric scheme of some kind, and this is increasingly the case, tell the funder exactly how you'll measure what you're doing according to the foundation's guidelines. If there is no format supplied, develop one.

I am astonished at how many proposals include nonsensical self-referencing metrics, along the lines of "We will measure our success using standard means of success measurement." OK, I'm exaggerating – but not much.

Most certainly, tell us about how your work will improve the lives of others. But, in addition, show us how you'll measure the impact. If you're the group trying to change state laws that lead to homelessness you can say, "We'll know we have succeeded if one of the four homeless services bills pending in our legislature passes within the next two years. And we'll count contact hours with members of the state legislature, and show a 25 percent increase in the number of articles that mention our work."

One group that my foundation recently funded with a multi-year, multi-million dollar grant gave me a proposal that showed 57 separate planned outcomes, and how each of those outcomes would be measured, so we would be able to recognize success when we saw it. Part of their reporting to us now includes spreadsheets that track each of those outcomes.

As you pause to stretch your weary fingers and tired

back from laboring over your proposal, bring yourself back to the reason you're doing your work. Connect with the core motivations and passions that keep you at it, day after day. Then pour that dedication, commitment, and hope for a better world into every syllable of your proposal. When you're finished, sit back and know that you've done all you could.

5

Sweaty Palms: In-Person Meetings

I am a great believer in shoe-leather philanthropy. People in the granting field can learn so much more by leaving the abstract world of proposals and meeting the people who are seeking funds. And for me, anyway, meeting grantees is the most fun a grantmaker can have.

In this chapter, we're going to cover the two most common kinds of interactions between grantseeker and funder: visits to funder offices, and site visits.

While it's perfectly possible to receive a grant without ever meeting the funder, and many grantees would be happy not to endure the stress and possibly tricky questions emanating from an in-person conversation, there are good reasons to have that meeting.

First of all, some funders really can't get comfortable with a new grantee or a new idea until they've interacted beyond the piles of paper. Basically, all you need to do in a meeting is explain yourself. And you should thank your lucky stars you have a chance to do so, instead of the funder tossing your proposal into the dreaded tall pile.

Second, there are some ideas and some pieces of nonprofit work that really have to be seen to be appreciated. Funders and grantseekers don't always agree on which projects those might be, and we'll get to that point a little later.

And finally, some grantmakers are required to meet the people they fund, so you really won't have a choice.

Whether the funder meeting is at your place or theirs, there are a few basics to start with. As I said earlier, some of this might seem painfully obvious, if not for my long experience demonstrating that some people need to be, well, reminded.

If you want to meet with a funder, here is Rule #1: Do. Not. Ever. Call. The. Funder. At. Home. If this seems obvious to you, my all-time record for outrageous, manners-impaired behavior is held by the man who called me at home at 7 a.m. – on Thanksgiving morning.

He was in town, kind of bored visiting his parents I think, and wanted to know if he could come over. I admit this is rather extreme, but over the years a number of grantees have felt welcome to contact me at home, and a few have showed up on my front porch.

I've thought and thought about this, and I'm just not able to come up with any reason for a person to ever penetrate the professional-personal barrier uninvited.

The second painfully obvious rule is about something that happens all the time. Don't give the funder short notice (15 minutes or even a week) that you want a meeting. Leaving aside my internal book of manners, it's simply impractical to expect a busy person to find meeting time on limited notice.

This is one that happens to me at least monthly: I get a call from someone who says he's "in town," and can he stop by. Usually, my answer is no, even if it's someone I want to meet. Think about it – do I want to hand over tens or hundreds of thousands of dollars to someone who demonstrates that he's not able to manage a simple calendar?

I'm going to leave the rest of the obvious rules for you to figure out for yourself, such as don't show up without an appointment, don't arrive late, and don't venture to the offices of a foundation in a Manhattan high-rise in torn jeans and a T-shirt (none of these examples are made up). In general, what this comes down to is, make a shining impression of your organization and you'll be just fine.

Now let's look more closely at the dynamics of visiting funders in their offices.

It may well happen that one of the foundations you've

applied to will contact you, asking you to come in for a meeting. The only possible answer to this, unless you're holding a winning lottery ticket when the call arrives, is "Yes".

You might be slightly flustered – after all, thousands if not tens of thousands of dollars could be at stake. So here's your checklist of issues to try to raise – you don't want to simply book the date and time, if it's possible to stay on the phone a bit longer.

You should ask, What's the purpose of the meeting? This might seem obvious, but finding out what the funder wants to know is vitally important. The response might be that she wants to have a general conversation about your proposal. But she might have something more specific in mind, like going over your budget, and it would be nice to be prepared.

Your second question is, Who should come to the meeting? Again it might be obvious, they are calling *you*. But if you're in a small organization, you might want to bring a board member or a person from your community. Or on the other end of the scale, if yours is a big group that works in a technical area or in science, you might want to bring along a staff scientist or other expert. Usually a huge delegation is a bad idea, but sometimes more than one person can strengthen your hand.

I have met with some volunteers, board chairs, and community people over the years that have really impressed, and sometimes moved me. It doesn't hurt to ask about including others, if the funder isn't far away or if your bank account can deal with a bit of travel.

Once the meeting has been set up, confirm it a week in advance. Recently, I received an email from a grantee, who at my invitation was coming from another state. She reconfirmed the date and time, mentioned who was coming, listed the things they hoped to discuss, and politely invited us (there were two people from my foundation in the meeting) to mention any other concerns we'd like addressed.

This is perfect. Her email created the meeting's agenda, and the grantee did a good job of maintaining control of the gathering without making me feel overpowered.

OK, so the time comes and there you are in the foundation waiting room. What is in your hand? And, no, I don't mean your briefcase. The only correct answer is, something to hand the funder that she hasn't seen before.

Not another proposal, unless that's the stated purpose of the meeting. And be wary of gifts – most of us in foundations feel a bit uncomfortable picturing the perp walk when we're indicted for taking bribes. (If you're a local group with T-shirts and caps, that might be OK, or perhaps a cookbook your organization has produced).

Especially if this is a first meeting, keep the geegaws to a minimum. What will suffice is a literature packet in a nice folder – maybe some newsletters and other publications. Please, just don't show up empty-handed. It is poor sales behavior to do that.

In some respects this meeting is a dress rehearsal for the board meeting: in this case you're playing the part of the staff person and the staff person is the board member, asking those probing questions.

It isn't easy to generalize about meetings with funders because the ones I've been in (from both sides of the transaction) vary. But some aspects of the meeting are fairly common. You are in the funder's offices for two reasons.

First, you want to give the foundation staff an opportunity to look you over. You want them to see that you're competent, that you know your stuff. You put a face on the verbiage, a voice to the issue.

Second, you're there to provide information for the staff person to use in figuring out if they want to take your proposal on – or later in the game, how they might handle your proposal in their board meeting.

When you sit down in the funder's conference room or office, and exchange the usual pleasantries we use to start the social engine, always begin with the same question: "Do you have some things you'd like to cover about our proposal, or would you like me to start with a few brief remarks about our work?"

There is a power dynamic here, and this question handles it. You take the initiative in framing the meeting in terms of the funder's needs, not yours. If you talk on and on before the funder gets to ask his list of questions, you might have to walk out the door having missed a great opportunity to fill in the blanks and correct misconceptions.

Therefore, your first task is to set up the agenda in terms of the funder's needs, because that person's needs are what count in this meeting. If the foundation staff person doesn't begin with questions, then you should give a presentation consisting of three things.

First, give a brief summary of your proposal, kind of a verbal LOI. There might be someone in the room who hasn't read your proposal, and in any event you want to refresh the memory of those who may have read 12 other proposals that morning. And based on my experience, let me remind you that you must be fluent in all the details of the proposal.

Second, describe anything that is new. Explain that you're updating the proposal since it was sent in, and offer to send this information in writing or even – please forgive me for saying this – rewrite the proposal. Unless you are meeting the day after the proposal arrived in the foundation's offices, you should always include an update – everyone likes to feel they have the most current information.

Third, offer to discuss or clarify any points in the proposed project that the funder is interested in. You are gently working here to elicit what the funder feels is weak or controversial about your proposal. You're looking to provide answers, but you aren't there to hold a debate.

It isn't advisable to ask if the funder likes or favors your proposal, or if they're going to recommend it. When people feel pushed, they tend to push back, which is just the dynamic you want to avoid. Assume your proposal has some life for that staff person; why else would you be in their office at the moment?

Once you've had the meeting and said your goodbyes, go over your notes carefully. When you send your thank-you note for the meeting – which in all instances you should do – it's also fine to recap the to-do list you took away from the meeting. So you might say, "Thanks for seeing us last Tuesday. We're going to be sending you the revised budget and a copy of our strategic plan, as we discussed, by the end of this week."

While debates rage in the manners columns of daily newspapers, in my opinion, thank-you's sent by email are fine.

■ Site Visits

More rarely, the funder will come to see you. It's too bad site visits are so infrequent, because funders learn best out of our offices. When you get that call or email announcing a visit, don't panic. Follow the suggestions above – try to pinpoint who is coming, what they want to get out of the meeting, and who in your organization they want to meet with.

Yes, do discard that stack of empty pizza boxes, but don't stress your staff with your nervousness or make them dress as if they're going to the prom. Confirm the meeting and your expectations in advance, and once again, be ready with that packet to hand to the funder as part of your greeting.

If, as is sometimes the case, a meal is involved, you might be asked to suggest a local restaurant. Be prepared with a few choices, which you can describe in diplomatic terms, like, "There's a good basic local seafood place two blocks away, and an Italian place around the corner that has white tablecloths at lunch."

Most people who are picking up the tab appreciate having the price range flagged in advance. And speaking of the tab, I know that some of my esteemed colleagues operate with different standards than I do, but in most cases, it is always the putative funder who pays. You might offer to pick up the check if you feel that's called for, but don't insist.

Also, be cautious about who comes to the meal. I was once at an organization's office in New York City and mentioned it was lunchtime. The two people in the meeting with me said "Great," and promptly invited all the other employees, 17 of them, to join us.

Leaving aside what that meal did to my budget, I didn't get any actual work done during the confusing and raucous meal ... to the group's detriment.

Assuming your organization runs programs or services, most funders will want to see, in action, what they might be funding . Over the years, I've met cowboy poets, participated in street demonstrations, cooked meals for homeless people, and collated mailings with volunteers.

One of the great blessings of my work has been meeting the people who dedicate their lives to helping others, often around their kitchen tables or in drab walk-up offices.

One big mistake grantseekers make – often because they've failed to do their homework to find out who's visiting them – is to mute the power and passion of their work. There's no doubt that taking a funder into the community means you can't control what happens. Someone may say something embarrassing. But we're adults and we can handle the unexpected.

I know that time and again I've fallen in love with groups because they let me meet their community people, volunteers, or those whom they serve. If you happen to meet the rare funder who will give you more than an hour and is interested in the realities of your work, take the risk and let your program shine.

In closing this chapter, let me suggest two ideas to help you induce funders to meet with you. I regret I don't have more.

First, make the offer to come by and meet the funder, or invite her to visit with your organization. Do this even if you don't want to, or you don't think the funder will accept.

A polite invitation can't hurt, most especially in the context of acknowledging a letter from a funder that says your Letter of Inquiry has been accepted and you're being invited to submit a full proposal. Just make sure your invitation for a visit is clear and brief. And only send one.

The second technique that has worked with me is to illustrate what a site visit might look like. In these days of $99 color printers, you can easily produce a letter showing the smiling faces of your volunteers or the beautiful setting around your program's field office, or the faces of the people who benefit from your group's efforts. A few times when I've been wavering about seeing people, framing this picture in my mind has helped to tip the balance in the grantee's favor. It can't hurt.

While there are the occasional difficult people seeking grants, I've found over the years of working as a grantmaker that the people asking us for support are inspiring, enjoyable folks who in many ways are motivated by an idealism that I share.

Busy funders, including me, are often difficult to meet with, yet the overwhelming majority of grantseekers are interesting and engaging people who should put their strongest asset forward: yourselves.

6

Making Sausage: How Foundation Staff and Boards Decide

Once quite a few years ago I was asked to guest-staff a foundation board meeting, while the person who held the job took a break.

I knew little about these funders and was fairly new to the field, but it was a chance to see some money flow to organizations I cared about. I worked for six months preparing a thick notebook – often called a docket in the foundation trade – that carefully supported my grant recommendations.

On the Saturday of the board meeting, I flew to a distant city where I was met by a liveried driver and shown to his limousine. He brought me to a large, paneled conference room in an office building where five businessmen in suits were seated. Each had a copy of the docket notebook in front of him ... unopened.

After introductions, the chairman asked me several general questions about a few of the proposed grants in the notebook. One hour and $2.2 million later, I was sent on my way back to the airport.

That's one stereotype of how foundations make decisions, and I've visited with a number that behave similarly. At the other end of the scale are foundations I've worked with, and still do, whose boards meet for days at a clip, poring over the details of each and every grant request with the greatest of care.

In the face of so much variation, what's a grantseeker to do? In this chapter, we're going to look at how foundation staff prepare themselves for board meetings, and how some boards decide what to fund. Our goal is less to study the habits of these strange birds, and more to understand how to maximize your chance of getting funded.

■ Foundation Staffing

Most foundations have no staff at all. Often a lawyer or bank trust officer handles the paperwork, or a family member takes care of things if the foundation represents family philanthropy. But here we're going to focus on those foundations large enough to have professional staff.

Someone – paid staff or bored lawyer – is going to have to screen the large number of incoming proposals to select the much smaller number that will receive concerted attention. If you discover you're one of the lucky few who has made the cut, what then?

■ Into the Black Hole

First we have to mention the unpleasant truth that in many cases you won't know if your proposal got past the first cursory screening, until many months later, when the process for that round of grants has ended.

Some foundations, especially larger ones, only send out notices *after* the board meets. In some instances, this is due to the short leash of the staff: the board needs to ratify all their decisions, even the negative ones.

So take it as a bad omen if there's a thundering silence after you've submitted your proposal. While I know of instances of people sending in proposals and simply receiving a check in the mail, it's not common, because most foundations need to know more about you in order to make a funding decision.

But say you received an acknowledgment card and haven't heard anything since. What can you do to find out what's going on, without annoying the person you are hoping will give you money?

Start with a fellow-sufferer. If the foundation publishes a grants list, and if you know or can introduce yourself to someone on that list, call up and ask for advice. You would have been well advised to make contact before you sent anything to the foundation. But even if you skipped that step, it's not too late to call a colleague and explain that you sent in a proposal but haven't heard anything. She might laugh and say, "Oh, it takes them six months to read anything, don't worry." Or she might have a clue about who to call and what to say.

If all else fails, call the funder and tell the truth: you sent in your material and are wondering if there's something you can or should do. I can promise you that the person who's paid to answer the foundation's phone continually fields a version of this call.

■ Position Papers and Context Statements

What is the program staff doing while you pace your office? If she's typical, she's doing several things. One is refining the foundation's grantmaking by creating position papers. In board meetings, my staff and I take careful note of what our board members say, and some of what we hear can turn into exploratory or issue papers.

Let's assume our guidelines have some language about supporting access to healthcare for all citizens in our state. In the board meeting, a member mentions an article she read about the problem of getting health care to the children of homeless families living in shelters. There is some discussion, including people disagreeing about what care is already made available and by whom.

During a lull in the conversation, I point out that this discussion is about an issue that fits well within our guidelines, and ask if the board would like to see some staff work on it.

The origin of this kind of staff investigation varies quite a bit. In larger foundations, there's often a formal staff-driven process for determining what will be explored and by whom. These investigations are how foundations learn, how they attempt to keep their guidelines relevant and fresh.

You as a grantseeker will sometimes learn of the process when out of the blue you get a call from some program officer wanting to ask you about the field you work in. Sometimes funders assemble formal panels, but often they just network around.

If you receive one of these investigatory calls, there's a mighty temptation to burble on grandly, feathering your own nest. This is understandable. You want this particular funder to be impressed with what you know, and how clear and helpful you are. You want to end up in their Rolodex with a notation as someone to call from time to time.

But you'll further your cause much more by doing the best selling of all – namely, becoming a trusted resource. If you're very fortunate, you might even have a hand in shaping how a foundation gatekeeper sees the world you work in. And sometimes that can result in money wending its way to causes you hold dear.

In addition to these "think pieces" or position papers, what else is going on inside the foundation? Most likely, the foundation staff are beginning to shape up their docket, often using the think pieces as templates. As your proposal rises in the pile, the staff person might give you a call with some questions that need clarifying, or want to know a few things that didn't appear in your proposal.

■ The Inner Sanctum

Foundation boards are as widely varied as the foundations they govern. Some boards consist of family members, spending out an ancestor's largess. Others are teams of experts. A number of boards mix and match, including family people, experts, lawyers, even politicians. Private foundations list their board members on their tax return each year, Form 990-PF, readily available online.

Scoping out the board can be useful. If your proposal is for funding lab work on anhydrous bisphenol molecules and you learn from your research that the board is composed of weighty chemists, you should write a technical proposal showing off your ability in the field. If you're writing to an ordinary family or non-technical people, put more of your energy into clear and effective communication. Conversations with previous grantees as well as the foundation's own staff will tell you what to expect.

Once the proposal is in, it's usually too late to make major revisions, so be sure of the board's make-up before you put fingers to keyboard.

The dynamic between foundation boards and their staff is a complex one. The staff have been working full time on the issues and proposals that end up in front of a board that might only meet once or twice a year.

The board's job is to be the keeper of the foundation's mission, to deploy money that best realizes its purpose. Yet they rely heavily on staff in many instances, especially if the board is composed of more general members of the public or a family.

When new staff start at our foundation, here is what I tell them about the decision-making process, and I think it applies in many foundations. The staff person comes into the board meeting having worked for months on their suite of recommended grants. They've met with the prospective grantees; there have been numerous phone calls, perhaps a site visit, possibly hours of research. The staff person has become an expert ... and an advocate.

During the board meeting, good board members will ask questions, poking at the staff with queries designed to find out two things. First, does that staff person really know what she's talking about? The board member wants to confirm that this recommendation comes from someone who has done her homework on the foundation's behalf.

Second, the board member is trying to figure out if this staff person is pushing the foundation in a new direction or otherwise subverting the guidelines. Many board members see their primary role as guardians of the vision of the foundation, so they're diligent in making sure that some aspect of a proposed grant won't be yanking the foundation off its tracks.

Under the best of circumstances, this dynamic between the board and staff can keep a foundation healthy and competent. Under other circumstances, the decision-making process can slide into debate and even, as I have witnessed, shouting, table-pounding, or tears.

The staff become frustrated at what they perceive as board members who resist change, or who are misunderstanding the staff's presentation. Board members may experience staff as promoting outsiders rather than supporting the board's decision-making. It is frequent for them to grumble that they're not paying staff to hassle them. "Who the heck are these people working for?" they ask.

For the decades I've been running foundations, I've had a rule with my staff during board meetings: they always have to sit where they can see me, and they need to look at me frequently, however painful that may be.

In the process of give-and-take with board members, it is understandable that sometimes the staff get carried away in their "explaining" of the proposed grant. When this happens, we have subtle signals to help each other. Mine is a near-imperceptible shake of my head. If this doesn't take *immediate* effect, I draw a horizontal line across my neck.

My invariable rule is, when the board is apparently deciding not to make a grant, the staff must instantly stop endorsing the proposal.

The central dynamic of a foundation board meeting is that despite months of concentrated work by staff, we will if need be toss proposed grants overboard – fast. Those staff who persist in pushing grants the board doesn't want to make are usurping the board's power, and are sometimes shown the door.

■ Singing For Your Supper

Some foundations invite those with pending proposals to make a presentation directly to the board. Years ago I myself received such an invitation. I awoke before dawn to drive through morning traffic to a nearby city for my big day, with $360,000 riding on my performance. No pressure.

In the early morning darkness I failed to see a pothole just as I was taking a sip of my coffee. The front of my shirt turned instant mocha. At the next exit, I drove off the highway to find a replacement, but not be late for my 9 a.m. meeting. I still have the strange polyester shirt I was able to locate in a variety store just opening. It's a good reminder of what grantees go through that funders don't even dream of. I think of that garment as my "$360,000 shirt."

If you're invited to appear before a board, aside from being careful with spills, you should interrogate the foundation's staff very carefully in advance, and do exactly and precisely what they tell you. The staff have a strong interest in your doing well and making them look good.

If they say, cover your three objectives in four minutes, don't talk about something else, for five. Here are other general guidelines for in-person interactions with foundation boards:

1) Take exactly the amount of time you're given, no more and no less. Practice until you can do it right.

2) Be polite, but not gushy. Obsequiousness is not conducive to a dignified impression.

3) If you're asked questions, answer succinctly and honestly. Arguing with foundation board members is only advised if your proposal is for support of Self-Destructors Anonymous.

4) Stay on the subject at hand, and only pass out materials you've been told by staff are welcome.

5) If you're asked to a meal, eat beforehand and just

pick at your plate. This will allow you to liberally visit your magic on the people around you, rather than wasting precious time tucking in the free food or being asked a question just as you fill your mouth with mashed potatoes.

Once the foundation board has met, all you can do is wait.

■ The Dénouement

At some point, you'll find out what happened to your funding request (a phone call is probably good news). Many foundations, once they have announced that you are to receive funding, will send a packet with instructions about grant compliance and reporting that you must fill out to receive the check.

For reasons I cannot fathom, there are a few grantees in every funding round that don't send the paperwork back. You train for years, run that Olympic race, win, and then don't show up for the gold?

This delay can be a problem for some funders who are making grants at the end of their fiscal year, and need to have the check in your account by a certain date. Don't look like a flake: read the paperwork carefully, get the signatures you need, and send the package back.

Unfortunately, things might turn out the other way. Even when you know you have strong support from the foundation's staff, it is the board that decides whether you get the grant. In a strange way, I'm proud of the weeping program staff I've had to comfort in the hallway after a board meeting when an excellent proposal was turned down – it is important that foundation staff are passionate about helping you.

But even after you've done everything just right, even when you know your work is the very best, even when you stayed up several nights rewriting your work to suit the funder's unorthodox requirements, you might still get turned down. It hurts.

If you have any kind of relationship with the foundation's staff, you might want to give a call, thank them for their presumed effort on your behalf, and ask if they can share anything with you that would shed light on the outcome. I advise you to use something very close to my language here: be gentle, succinct, and then get off the phone.

You might well be able to learn something, make a few changes, and try again. You might be able to have that staff person tell her colleague across town when she calls about your new proposal that you're a good person to work with. At all costs, avoid arguing or castigating. It isn't conducive to building the kind of relationship that produces funding.

7

Reports: What to Do After You're Funded

After you've been told the fabulous news about your grant award, and the champagne has gone flat in your Dixie cups, I recommend you do three things:

1) Sit down with a tasteful piece of stationery or a cheery card, and send a thank you note to the funder. You don't need to gush or grovel, but hearty thanks are an excellent way to cement your new relationship. Have a board member sign, or have all the staff in your small office write something, or send some other token of genuine appreciation. Even an email is OK, but just do it.

2) Then put the funder on your mailing list –

prudently. What you don't want to do is behave like the funder's kids – you cash the check and aren't heard from again. And you want to avoid the funder looking at your material 11 months hence and saying, "Who?"

Instead, gently and judiciously keep your group in front of the funder. Maintain that feeling of connectedness and create the impression that you're all in this together.

If you have a monthly or quarterly newsletter, put the funder on the list for a free lifetime subscription. I don't actually think the funder should have to pay extra for information, but one group we recently funded with over three-quarters of a million dollars did indeed charge me $25 for their materials. We live in a diverse world.

If your organization holds events, and the funder is local, make sure she is invited to every public event. Don't expect her to attend, but people like to feel included, and events illustrate your group's activities.

3) Take an empty file folder, label it "Foundation Reports," and place it right on your desk. As successes or interesting events in your organization are documented, remember to slip a copy into that folder. News clippings are an obvious choice, as are attractive invitations to events, concise reports, and work products like published data and articles.

When it comes time to report on a grant, reach into this file, go back 12 months in what you pull out, and walk to the photocopier. A third of your reporting work may be finished.

A major aspect of reporting is the financial accounting. There may be some person on the planet who likes this part of the grantmaking process, but I haven't met her. Yet this section of the report is central, because the law and common sense say, if someone gives you tax-subsidized money, you need to show exactly what you spent it on.

This is one time when you should suppress every bit of your creativity and do exactly what the funder says in his reporting requirements. There's a good chance that the financial part of the reporting specifications was written by a CPA or a lawyer, and you cross those kinds of people at your peril.

I want to suggest three reasons for paying close attention to grant reporting.

First, most groups hope to receive repeat funding. The group that is late or fails to comply with reporting requirements will be on shaky ground for a renewal grant. And even if you know you're not going to receive a second grant from this funder, due to certain rules and restrictions, you still have to assume that funders talk to each other, because we do.

So when I run into a colleague and he says he has a proposal from your group and notices we used to fund them, you don't want me to say either "Who?" or even worse, "Oh yeah, those folks never reported." Reports are a way of building relationships, and *relationships underpin all grantmaking.*

Second, you might actually teach the funder something. Let them know how the grant turned out, what was a great success and what was unanticipated. Share the lessons. We funders study at the University of Grantees. In my foundation, the board is very interested in how their grants turn out, and they enjoy reports, or at least summaries.

Finally, even though some might smirk at this, I think you can learn from your own reporting. Sitting down and summarizing what you did over the past year is an excellent way to improve your work. It forces you to step back from the daily struggle and think about what you accomplished, what your greatest challenges were, and what you've learned.

And as long as you're going through the trouble of writing the report to comply with grant terms, get some mileage out of it. Share the document with your own board and staff members – give them an opportunity to feel proud too.

8

You Really Can Do It

Many years ago I found myself trudging along in a Central American tropical forest with a group of funders and journalists. Our host was a prominent scientist who was conducting fieldwork in the area. As we squatted in a little clearing, taking a break from our hike, one of the journalists asked the famous biologist to explain his success in securing funding for his work over so many years.

The scientist slowly finished folding up his snake capturing bag, looked over at me and said, "Oh, funders are like monkeys. You can study their habits and learn to manipulate them."

Guilty as charged. Some days, I just want to fund everyone.

The other night while I was fixing dinner, the announcer on public radio mentioned a name that seemed somehow familiar. As the broadcast unfolded, I realized I had – 25 years earlier – spoken with the man being interviewed, when he sent me his first funding proposal. After decades of working on this one project, he had finally succeeded.

It nearly brought tears to my eyes, thinking about him and all the people I'd met over the years who had stayed the course with their work, always to benefit others, and usually at some real cost to themselves. Getting to know the inner character of these individuals – their sheer discipline, their big-heartedness, their ability to withstand defeat time and again – is unquestionably the best part of being a funder.

In closing, let me share three final thoughts.

First, the fundraisers I trust most are the unassuming non-experts who infect people around them with authentic passion. Don't let the pressure of meeting deadlines and budgets separate you from your dedication. Your commitment is the best tool you have.

Second, don't forget that foundation grants are only one of a broad range of ways of stabilizing your organization; a handful of grants is not a safe funding base. An organization that stays small but totally owned by its members or clients is the one that will make it in the long run.

And third, don't forget that we funders seem

important because we control one resource so completely. But in fact, real change in the world comes not from grandiose granting guidelines, but from the perseverance and imagination of those trying to penetrate the granting process in order to do good for others. Those are the truly important people. And to them I send my sincerest gratitude and respect.

Good luck.

PART TWO

The Grantseeker's Reality Check

The Grantseeker's Reality Check

A Six things you can do to help your proposal make the first cut.

B Eight red flags foundations are wary of.

C Seven reasonably easy things you can do to improve your proposal.

D Five mistakes too many applicants make.

E Five questions you can expect to be asked about your proposal.

F Don't be too concerned about these peripheral matters.

G Five things you should never do when approaching foundations.

H Five questions to ask when meeting with the program officer.

I A short list of unequivocal don'ts.

J Six ways to help assure repeat funding.

Many years ago, my wife and I lived in a little house next to a small river in Northern California. Late one night, in the midst of a blowing storm, a neighbor came pounding on our door, yelling for us to get up and run, because the now raging river had jumped its banks upstream and was heading right for us, over land.

We were forced to act out one of those party quizzes – what you would take with you if you only had seconds to spare: what do you *really* care about? As we dashed ahead of the dark oily water, we grabbed our son, the dog, the cat – and the funding proposal my wife had been working on for the past two months. Nothing else was more important.

While most proposals don't carry life and death weight, they often feel that way. Remembering that cold night, I've thought about how I can help you with the grantseeking process.

I've noticed over time that some questions come up again and again, because they're on many people's minds and they apply to many foundations. So I've made clusters of those questions here, along with what I think is the best advice for handling each issue. If you find yourself baffled, just turn to the section that fits your predicament, locate the question, and try out my advice.

Oh yes, you might want to keep your proposal draft by your bedside.

Six Things You Can Do To Help Your Proposal Make The First Cut

1. Write a compelling summary.

What if you knew that huge sums of money, perhaps a month or two of your organization's payroll, were riding on 200 or 400 words? Wouldn't you pay scrupulous attention to that writing? Your proposal will only get read if the summary provides a reason for the program officer to dig deeper. Fuss over the summary until it sparkles.

2. List concrete, specific outcomes of your work.

People want to know exactly what they are going to get for their money. That's why so many of the things we buy come in transparent packaging. Your proposal should be a clear container that shows exactly what will result from the funder's investment. Concrete measurable results provide core reasons for funders to support you.

3. Connect each step of your work with your goals.

Many proposals fail to show how specific actions will lead directly to meeting goals. Strong proposals are like railroad bridges – they have steel girders connecting every point. Most often, proposal writers fail to make those connections because the relationship between what they want and what they do seems obvious to them. It needs to be spelled out.

4. Present a budget in standard format that is legible and patently sensible.

People who have never used a spreadsheet as well as those who live and breathe spreadsheets can be equally injurious to explaining your money plan. Spreadsheet jockeys need to be kept from creating dense forests of tiny numbers. But also don't let someone take their maiden spreadsheet voyage creating the budget that will be vetted by a foundation's experts. And make sure everything in the proposal is accounted for in the budget. Conversely, omit items in the budget that are not fully explained in the proposal narrative.

5. Get the proposal in early.

Ostentatiously beating the deadline gives the impression that you can plan well and get things done. The reality of foundation deadlines is that if your proposal arrives early, it will stand out, because most proposals arrive at the last moment.

6. Offer to meet. Once.

Let the funder know you would be glad to come by and talk about your work, and if appropriate, bring other staff or board members. If the funder says OK, set up the meeting on their terms. If they're reluctant, let it drop, so you don't provide a reason for the funder to stop taking your calls.

Eight Red Flags
Foundations Are Wary Of

1. Lobbying or political work.

While some funders will support lobbying, many private foundations are wary of work that attempts to influence legislation. If you're engaging in such work, you should have a sophisticated understanding of the lobbying rules, and be able to articulate why your organization – and its donors – are on safe ground. It's not a bad idea to show up with a legal opinion, in writing. And, adequately research the funder's grants list to learn what they will and won't tolerate.

2. High staff turnover.

Some nonprofits can't provide competitive salaries and fringe benefits and as a result experience high turnover in staff. Funders know that higher than usual turnover, particularly among top positions, correlates with problems in mission drift and steady funding. If you can show a stable board, or consistency in mid-level positions, it will reassure funders who are considering investing in your group.

3. Huge gap between top and bottom salaries.

Some funders will look to see if your top people are making very large salaries. One measure is the multiplier between the top and bottom people on your pay scale. Is your CEO paid 30 times the amount of an administrative assistant?

A way to figure out if your policies are fair – and to justify them to an inquiring funder – is to check the want ads and document that your pay range is comparable for similar positions. Having a written personnel policy that provides an objective series of pay steps tied to employee evaluation can also show that you're being reasonable.

4. Board composed mostly of famous people who are not active.

There is nothing wrong with having well-known people on your board. What may look suspicious are long lists of "letterhead activists" who lend their names but don't show up. This will raise legitimate questions about who's actually governing your organization. Be prepared to give examples of how famous people on your letterhead *are* involved in making decisions.

5. Board composed of staff.

Most funders subscribe to the traditional model of a

creative tension between volunteer board members and the paid staff who carry out their policies. When the paid staff dominate the board, the volunteer dynamic disappears, and not only will funders raise their eyebrows, but some state attorneys general may as well.

6. Extensive, expensive media strategies.

Let's say you decide that the best way to address your organization's issue is to "educate the public." To achieve your end, you select TV and full-page newspaper ads, which of course require the services of pricey experts and very steep placement costs.

If you invest a lot of money in something with a seemingly intangible outcome, come into the funder's office with an analysis that shows why a media campaign is for you the best strategy for success. Also show that you have specific plans to measure the campaign's effectiveness.

7. First time film makers/writers.

It's common for funders to receive proposals from those who want to create a film or book about a problem they're passionate about. Foundation people know that absent a track record, these projects are frequently abandoned or changed drastically in mid-course. If you are seeking funding for creative work, it's important to put together a portfolio of past experience and success.

8. "Hired gun" fundraisers.

There's nothing wrong with bringing in an outside fundraising expert, especially for specialized projects like capital or endowment campaigns. Yet this field is famous for problems ranging from inefficiency to criminal activity. Be ready with the details of the outsider's credentials, and prepare specific information on how you'll maintain control of the consultant's activities. Also show how your arrangement with the fundraiser complies with relevant professional ethics codes as well as your state's laws.

Seven Reasonably Easy Things You Can Do to Improve Your Proposal

1. Go on a cliché and gobbledygook hunt.

Funders are as guilty as any group of lapsing into jargon and stylish language. The trouble is, fashionable terms like "shifting the paradigm" or "taking down the silos" might not be clear and could in fact mislead the reader. And if the reader has difficulty understanding, she'll be more likely to start staring out the window.

2. Use short sentences, active voice, and lots of white space.

Successful proposals follow many of the rules of popular journalism, and for the same reasons. They strive to be accessible and even compelling by letting combinations of words create an image in the reader's mind, and in the best of circumstances, mobilizing the reader's emotions towards a goal. In your case, the goal is the awarding of a grant, nothing more.

3. Paint word pictures that draw the reader in.

Some proposal writers lecture and wag their fingers at the reader. Others become captive of their field's intricacies. While technical proposals being read by qualified readers can safely use formal language, most proposal writers should pay as much attention to the narrative of their proposal as any short story writer.

4. Write as much from your heart as from your head.

Misguided high school English teachers have ruined too much persuasive prose by requiring a dispassionate, objective-sounding voice. A proposal writer should be close enough to the work and the people who do it to infect the reader with the enthusiasm and dedication of those front line people. Analysis without feeling just isn't moving.

5. Have a good friend edit your prose.

The harder you work on your proposal, the more difficult it may be to see the gaps in logic, redundancies, and failures to be clear. To fix this you need two things: a good editor, and a willingness to accept a critique of your work as help, not a personal attack.

6. Talk with successful grantees of that foundation.

People in nonprofits are part of a culture that values helping others, so asking colleagues to tell you about their experience with a funder doesn't have to be seen by them as helping a competitor, especially when you reciprocate. Asking colleagues for assistance has the added advantage of building the kinds of alliances and networks that help everyone to succeed.

7. When in doubt, don't.

So often, in the rush and stress of completing a funding request, the proposal writer will be faced with decisions about what to include. There is a natural but counterproductive tendency to pile on information, perhaps with the thought that bulk is impressive. The end result of these poor editing choices is a mammoth and dense proposal that works against the goal of creating enthusiasm for the work.

Five Mistakes Too Many Applicants Make

1. Talking mainly about problems, not solutions.

Grantseekers sometimes confuse writing proposals with authoring pamphlets meant to educate and mobilize the public. Your proposal should show that you're familiar with the details of the issue, but most of a good proposal will focus on exactly what you're going to do about the problem.

2. Describing specific problems with general solutions.

A proposal will succeed to the extent it provides a clear picture of what will be done about the issue being addressed. Too often proposal writers pour their hearts into the details of the problem, and then resort to vague generalities about their actual activities.

This lack of concrete action in a proposal might result simply from the proposal writer not having a clear picture of what's being done by others in her organization. Much worse, it might mean the group needs to slow down the

119

fundraising until they have done a better job of strategic planning.

3. Prolific use of buzzwords and jargon.

Some proposal writers confuse density with erudition. What sells the work to funders is clear, simple prose that tells a story or paints a picture. Vague claims, fuzzy or trendy language, and obscure terms don't impress funders – quite the contrary.

4. Budgets that don't add up.

It seems so obvious, but enough proposals arrive on the desks of foundation executives with math mistakes to make it worth pointing out how much these careless errors undermine credibility. The budget should not only add up, it also has to support the logic of the proposal's narrative. Therefore a $100,000 budget to reconstruct 16 flooded houses won't make sense, nor will $700,000 to hire two new staff.

5. Parroting the funder's guidelines without linking them to the work.

It's difficult to understand why so many people think that pasting phrases from the funder's guidelines into their proposal will unlock the money box. If the funder says they seek to support people working to improve the health of city children, don't tell the funder that your organization exists "to improve the health of city children." All successful proposals need to fit within the foundation's guidelines, but detailing how and why they fit is the key to success, not simply showing you have read the funder's website.

Five Questions You Can Expect to be Asked About Your Proposal

1. "What will you do if we only support part of your request?"

Foundations are wary of all-or-nothing funding strategies, especially when they're pressed by more requests than they can fund. Be ready with a credible fallback position that shows how your work will go forward with partial funding.

2. "What will you do if you don't reach your funding goal?"

You won't always reach your fundraising goal. Perhaps the portion you projected from local businesses or from special events didn't materialize.

Funders want assurances that their investment in your project will be worthwhile even if you have to scale back your plans. Detail concrete, specific, and positive options in your preparation.

For example, you can say that you'll cover less territory or take more time if funds come in slower than you had hoped.

3. "Why did you choose these strategies?"

More than a few funders look past the overarching goal you're trying to achieve to the strategies and tactics you'll be using. When this question comes up, be ready with a clear accounting of why you chose your strategies, emphasizing their suitability for your particular set of circumstances.

4. "What will the situation you're addressing look like in 3/5/10 years?"

More than a few foundation boards are encouraging their staff to show how their grantmaking today will play out in the future – for the foundation, for the organization receiving funds, and for the people being served.

Foundations are increasingly doing the kind of long-range planning they prescribe for their grantees. You aren't being asked to predict the future. Rather, it's an opportunity for you to demonstrate that your current work is solidly connected to real results. You'll also do yourself a favor by emphasizing that your group intends to stay engaged for the long haul.

5. "Tell me about this project."

It's not that uncommon to have a meeting with an organization's representative who can't talk in detail about the proposed work. This unfamiliarity seems to happen more often with larger groups.

Any number of times I've found myself talking with a representative who knows less than I do about the details of the proposal on the table. If you want to send a head honcho or board person to meet with a funder, either brief them very well, or include someone in the delegation who knows the proposal *cold*.

Don't Be Too Concerned About These Peripheral Matters

1. Letters of reference.

Some funders ask for letters of reference, which you should include. But if they're not required, references rarely do anything for the success of the proposal. To my knowledge, there's not a single instance of a grant request including a letter suggesting that funding be denied.

Use references when they add a specific piece of information that needs to come from an outsider. For example, if you're asking for funding to construct post-disaster housing, you could include a letter from a previous project thanking you for getting solid structures up on time and under budget.

2. Fancy fonts and colorful papers.

Proposals are read for content. Program officers have

already seen every type of ornate paper and binder. In many foundations, proposals are photocopied, which means colored or odd-sized papers end up being presented to the decision-makers looking shabby. Stick with professional, dignified, and simple presentations unless yours is an art project where showing off your creative prowess is part of the funding request. This same advice goes for electronic submissions – form and format should facilitate, not impede, communication.

3. Piles of newspaper clippings.

Sometimes clips are useful. But the mere mention of an organization in a long article doesn't add to the funding decision. Clips should say something specific that connects to your organization's work. And clippings shouldn't be tossed into the package, but rather mounted on plain paper along with an explanation of why that information has been included.

Five Things You Should Never Do When Approaching Foundations

1. Tell the funder to change their guidelines to fit what you do.

People carried away with the importance of their work sometimes forget when to turn off their advocacy. Your job in raising money is to find a funder whose work fits yours. If you're told that there is no fit, look elsewhere.

2. Ask the funder to help you write your proposal.

For a funder who raises a question about a particular aspect of your proposal, there's nothing wrong with asking her if expressing it differently might help. But asking general questions about what you have to say to unlock the cash box will most likely cause the funder to avoid talking with you, a deadly situation in fundraising.

3. Ask the funder to recommend other funders.

The one colleague reference that counts with funders is when they see who already gave you a grant. If you ask for the names of possible donors before the funder has made a decision to fund you, you're showing that you are at best inexperienced and at worst lazy.

There are few funders who will welcome being asked to speculate, do your research for you, or share their Rolodex. Let your list of supporters do the talking.

4. Ask for an "emergency" grant.

A very small number of funding sources provide emergency funding – and even then under rather specific conditions. In almost all other instances, declaring your situation an emergency portrays your organization as unstable, a bad bet for an investment.

5. Process your emotions with the funder.

It is only human to feel disappointment and even outrage when you've worked hard and experienced rejection. Yet I am astonished that some applicants feel the need to call or send me an email to vent – sometimes in blistering language – their unhappiness.

If there was a specific action taken by someone in the grantseeking process that you want to identify, for example if the program officer left out half of your proposal, go ahead and point it out if you want to. But there's little to be gained and quite a bit to be lost by slamming the person who probably worked hard to help you. Find an outlet for your feelings that won't burn bridges to your organization's funding future.

Five Questions to Ask When Meeting with the Program Officer

1. "Are there things I can add that will strengthen my proposal?"

You can't just come out and say, "How do I get money around here?" It's better to couch your question in terms of the proposal, and what steps you can take to make it better. Be sure to take meticulous notes. Having asked the program officer what to do, you'd better do it.

2. "Do you see things in my proposal that could be left out in a revised version?"

This is the flip side of the first question: you're asking as directly as possible how to cast the proposal in a way that will play best in that foundation. And when the funder suggests omitting your most favorite prose, don't argue. The goal isn't literary debate, but success in obtaining funds.

3. "Do you think I'm asking for the right amount of money?"

One of the most difficult items to figure out is how much to ask for. Sometimes I wonder if people have confused my foundation with the state lottery. But it's equally common for people to ask for far less than they should.

A few years ago, a group asking us for $100,000 received over $2 million. Just try to state your question as a request for advice, not asking the program officer to do your work for you, which could cause offense.

4. "Is there anything else I can do that would help you in your deliberations?"

This isn't quite the same as the first and second questions, which are focused on revising the proposal. In this instance you're asking if there's additional material the program officer would like to see, or share with her board.

Sometimes I'm reviewing a proposal and there's an area I'm not quite getting. I might ask for more backup information or samples of work product, or testimonials from recipients of the program's services.

5. "Can you give me an estimate of the timeframe for this proposal?"

This is more than a polite version of, "When do I get

the money?" You can receive valuable information if you listen carefully. You might learn that the program officer is thinking about deferring your proposal, or fast-tracking it. You might hear that currently there's a logjam of funding possibilities, leading to the choice of your receiving less money now or more later on (I face this issue all the time, and try to bring grantees into the decision).

Be aware, however, that some funders are reluctant to reveal their timetable, because experience has taught that they can be mightily harassed by anxious grant-seekers. So if you get a vague response to the timing question, let it drop.

A Short List of Unequivocal Don'ts

1. Never claim to be unique.

2. Don't claim to be a demonstration project unless you're using that phrase in the rather narrow technical sense and can prove it.

3. Don't rely on spellcheck or the purported ability of spreadsheet programs to add figures.

4. Never criticize the competition.

5. Avoid jokes and sarcasm, slang, and most technical words and terms of art.

6. Don't use colored paper or scented cover letters (I'm not making this up).

Six Ways to Help Assure Repeat Funding

1. Get your reports in on time.

Here is a chance to demonstrate competence, respect, good planning, and success. When you force the funder to chase you to comply with the contract you signed, you're establishing a counter-productive dynamic. Most funders have long memories.

2. Provide all the information that is requested.

The funder has a reason for asking that you answer certain questions – usually because they're comparing your success with that of others. You want to shine here, not end up as a blank box on a chart that goes to the foundation's board. Most commonly, financial information is missing or incomplete, depriving the funder of a key ingredient in seeing your achievements.

3. Put the funder on your mailing list.

Without getting into annoying over-communication,

make sure the funder doesn't forget who you are and why they made the grant. This is especially significant in multi-year funding. You don't want the foundation to look at your renewal request and say, "Who?"

4. Send a thank you note.

There is no need to gush or order flowers. Since the funder just worked on your behalf, letting her know that you recognize and appreciate her advocacy solidifies the feeling of relationship that's central to good fundraising. Buying a package of thank-you notes while you're waiting to hear about pending grant requests is a good way to keep your morale up.

5. Show that you did what you said you would do.

No matter what grant report format you're given, you need to base the content of your report on your proposal – the place where you wrote down exactly what you were planning to do. Having committed yourself to doing various things, you should methodically demonstrate that you did in fact do what you promised – and the foundation paid for.

6. Explain why you didn't do what you said you would do.

We live in an imperfect world: few things turn out exactly as we hope. Don't duck talking about what was unexpected. Point out what happened differently from what you had planned or hoped for, and give specific reasons why this was the case. Don't make excuses, just be matter-of-fact about the various outcomes, both planned for and not.

ACKNOWLEDGMENTS

The enjoyment of writing this book was greatly increased by the help of a number of people. Gary Cohen, Chris Desser, Susan Golden, and Francis Pandolfi all read early drafts of the book and offered astute comments.

Oran Hesterman shared bona fide wisdom as the book neared completion, and Ted Smith not only poured through the draft, but generously contributed his acumen to the Foreword. This book never would have come about if my old friend and colleague Andy Robinson hadn't suggested it.

While these folks helped me out, they bear no responsibility for any of the book's shortcomings.

I want to express my gratitude to the several foundations where I have worked since 1978. Notably, the boards of directors and staff of the CS Fund and the Cedar Tree Foundation have my lasting thanks. It is important to note, however, that this book is my own work product that does not reflect any involvement or endorsement from these funders.

A writer dreams of an editor like Jerry Cianciolo of Emerson and Church. Jerry labored with endless patience to bring out my best qualities and save me from my worst. He lifted my spirits through seemingly endless revisions with his wry humor and cosmic fortitude.

My children teach me why it is worth trying to make the world better, and my wife Mary shows me how one person really does make a difference.

And finally, I want to thank the thousands of grantseekers and grantees who, over many years, have provided endless inspiration and hope.

Winchester, Mass. Marty Teitel

ABOUT THE AUTHOR

Martin Teitel is Executive Director of the Cedar Tree Foundation, a private foundation. Previously he served as Senior Fellow and Executive Director of the CS Fund, a philanthropic foundation, and also Western Field Director for a public charity, The Youth Project. Teitel is currently on the steering committee of the Sustainable Agriculture and Food Systems Funders, as well as a committee of the Environmental Grantmakers Association. Previously he served on the management board of the National Network of Grantmakers, and on various committees of the Council on Foundations.

Teitel's nonprofit experience includes working as president of the Council for Responsible Genetics, a regional director of the Council on Economic Priorities, and several positions with the American Friends Service Committee, including Director of Asia Programs, Director of Overseas Refugee Programs, Indochina Commissioner, and Laos Field Director.

He has served on numerous non-profit boards and committees, and is currently on the board of directors of the Indigenous Peoples Council on Biocolonialism.

Teitel has a Ph.D. in philosophy from the Graduate School of the Union Institute, an MSW from San Diego

State University, and a BA in philosophy from the University of Wisconsin (Madison). He is a field education supervisor for the Harvard Divinity School.

Teitel is married to the Rev. Mary J. Harrington and has three children. He was born in New Jersey in 1945.

ALSO BY MARTIN TEITEL

Rain Forest In Your Kitchen:
The Hidden Connection Between Extinction
and Your Supermarket
Island Press, 1992, ISBN 1559631538

The Ownership of Life:
When Patents and Values Clash,
Co-authored with Hope Shand
Institute for Agriculture & Trade Policy, 1998,
ASIN B0006RS676

Genetically Engineered Food:
Changing the Nature of Nature,
Co-authored with Kimberly A. Wilson
Park Street Press, Second Edition 2001,
ISBN 0892818883

Martin Teitel is also the author of numerous
articles and book chapters on environmental,
human rights and philosophical issues.

Selected Books from Emerson & Church

Raising Thousands (if Not Tens of Thousands) of Dollars with Email
Madeline Stanionis, 120 pp., $24.95, 1889102059

At heart, raising money with email is all about building your list, using timing to your advantage, crafting a series of coherent messages, presenting your email in a visually appealing way, and carefully observing your returns for clues to guide your future efforts. Do this as Stanionis advises and you don't have to be the American Red Cross or the Salvation Army to raise a hefty amount of money.

Raising More Money with Newsletters Than You Ever Thought Possible
Tom Ahern, 128 pp., $24.95, 1889102075

Today, countless organizations are raising more money with their newsletter than with traditional mail appeals. And after reading Tom Ahern's riveting book, it's easy to understand why. Great newsletters have much more going for them. The essence of *Raising More Money with Newsletters Than You Ever Thought Possible* centers around seven fatal flaws. Eliminate them and your newsletter can become a powerful money raiser.

Raising $1,000 Gifts by Mail
Mal Warwick, 112 pp. $24.95, ISBN 1889102091

Whoever heard of raising $1,000 gifts (not to mention $3,000, $4,000, and $5,000 gifts) by mail? That's the realm of personal solicitation, right? Not exclusively, says Mal Warwick. Are you skeptical? Consider just one mailing. A total of 2,352 pieces were mailed to donors who had given $100 or more. This small mailing generated $148,000. Even more impressive, the mailing garnered 54 gifts that topped $1,000!

The Relentlessly Practical Guide to Raising Serious Money
David Lansdowne, 240 pp., $24.95, ISBN 1889102199

Why of all the hundreds of fund raising books available did AmeriCorps Vista, with offices throughout the U.S., single out this book as the premier book on the subject and provide a copy to thousands of its staff? Simply because no other writer in the field is as succinct, yet comprehensive as David Lansdowne. Nor do others have his trademark gift of extracting the essence of a technique and illuminating it in unfailingly clear prose.

INDEX

Copies of this book, and others
from the publisher, are available at discount
when purchased in quantity for staff,
boards of directors, or volunteers.

Emerson
& Church
PUBLISHERS

P.O. Box 338 • Medfield, MA 02052
Tel. 508-359-0019 • Fax 508-359-2703
www.emersonandchurch.com